THE GIFT OF HOPE

Cover and interior design by George Corsillo/Design Monsters
Cover and spine photo © Rick Wilking/Reuters/Corbis

Sellers Publishing, Inc.
161 John Roberts Road, South Portland, Maine 04106
For ordering information:
(800) 625-3386 Toll free
(207) 772-6814 Fax
Visit our Web site: www.sellerspublishing.com
E-mail: rsp@rsvp.com

ISBN: 13: 978-1-4162-0798-6

10 9 8 7 6 5 4 3 2 1

Printed and bound in China.

THE GIFT OF HOPE

The Words Of

BARACK OBAMA

SELLERS
PUBLISHING

AMERICAN DREAM

"I am the son of a black man from Kenya and a white woman from Kansas . . .

(Continued)

. . . I was raised with the help of a white grandfather who survived a Depression to serve in Patton's Army during World War II and a white grandmother who worked on a bomber assembly line at Fort Leavenworth while he was overseas. I've gone to some of the best schools in America and lived in one of the world's poorest nations.

I am married to a black American who carries within her the blood of slaves and slaveowners — an inheritance we pass on to our two precious daughters. I have brothers, sisters, nieces, nephews, uncles and cousins, of every race and every hue, scattered across three continents, and for as long as I live, I will never forget that in no other country on Earth is my story even possible."

"We live in a time when our destinies are shared. But our destinies will be written by us, not for us. Now, it falls to us to get to work."

SEPTEMBER 25, 2008

"America is your voice,
America is your dream,
America is your light of justice."

OCTOBER 2, 2007

"Don't let people talk you into doing what's easy or comfortable. Listen to what's inside of you and decide what it is that you care about so much that you're willing to risk it all."

MAY 19, 2007

"I looked at the world as a young man and I wanted to make a difference."

JULY 26, 2007

"Challenge yourself."

"I've seen my wife, Michelle, the rock of the Obama family, juggling work and parenting with more skill and grace than anyone I know."

SEPTEMBER 20, 2008

"You look at your children and you know that they're looking back at you and they're saying, 'You're going to take care of me, aren't you?' That's our job, to keep them healthy and to keep them safe, and to let them dream as big as their dreams will take them."

FEBRUARY 4, 2009

"We are Americans. We do the improbable. We beat great odds. We rally together to meet whatever challenge stands in our way. That's what we've always done — and it's what we must do now. For the sake of our economy, our security, and the future of our planet, we must end the age of oil in our time."

AUGUST 4, 2008

"Cultivating empathy, challenging yourself, persevering in the face of adversity — these are qualities that dare us to put away childish things. They are qualities that help us grow."

MAY 19, 2007

"You know, Dr. King once said that the arc of the moral universe is long, but that it bends toward justice. But what he also knew was that it doesn't bend on its own. It bends because each of us puts our hands on that arc and bends it in the direction of justice."

APRIL 4, 2008

DREAM

"We are the United States of America and there isn't any dream beyond our reach, any obstacle that can stand in our way, when we recognize that our individual liberty is served, not negated, by a recognition of the common good."

FEBRUARY 12, 2009

"Our future is what we build it to be."

MARCH 23, 2009

"We have a lot of work left to do. It's work that will take time and it will take effort. But the United States of America, I believe, will see a better day. We will rebuild a stronger nation. And we will endure as a beacon for all those weary travelers beyond our shores who still dream that there's a place where all this is possible."

APRIL 29, 2009

"I want you to know that the world will be what you make of it. You can choose to build new bridges instead of building new walls. You can choose to put aside longstanding divisions in pursuit of lasting peace. You can choose to advance a prosperity that is shared by all people and not just the wealthy few."

APRIL 7, 2009

FAITH

"I'm a person of deep faith, and my religion has sustained me through a lot in my life."

APRIL 15, 2008

"Even in the hardest times, against the toughest odds, we've never given in to pessimism; we've never surrendered our fates to chance; we have endured; we have worked hard; we sought out new frontiers."

APRIL 27, 2009

AMERICAN DREAM

"No matter what we look like or where we come from or who our parents are, each of us should have the opportunity to fulfill our God-given potential. Each of us should have the chance to achieve the American Dream."

JULY 13, 2008

"I'm reminded of words President Kennedy spoke in another time of uncertainty. 'Do not pray for easy lives. Pray to be stronger men. Do not pray for tasks equal to your powers. Pray for powers equal to your tasks.'

America, we will prove equal to this task."

FEBRUARY 14, 2009

"I've been working my entire adult life to help build an America where social justice is being served and economic justice is being served; an America where we all have an equal chance to make it if we try. That's the America I believe in."

JULY 14, 2008

"I can promise you this —
there will be brighter days ahead."

MARCH 18, 2009

"True security only comes
with liberty and justice."

APRIL 17, 2009

"I think the most important thing to start with is dialogue."

APRIL 7, 2009

"Patriotism in my mind [is] not just a love of America in the abstract, but a very particular love for, and faith in, the American people. That is why our heart swells with pride at the sight of our flag; why we shed a tear as the lonely notes of Taps sound."

JUNE 30, 2008

"Even the most painful note can be followed by joy."

"I'm standing here today . . . because of what my mother and grandmother did for me — because of their hard work and sacrifice and unflagging love. That's why all of us are here today — because of the women who came before us."

SEPTEMBER 20, 2008

"Real change is finally giving our kids everything they need to have a fighting chance in today's world. That begins with recognizing that the single most important factor in determining a child's achievement is not the color of their skin or where they come from; it's not who their parents are or how much money they have. It's who their teacher is. . . . After all, I have two daughters. I know what their teachers mean to them."

JULY 13, 2008

"Everything we do and everything I do is subject to improvement. Michelle reminds me every day how imperfect I am."

FEBRUARY 5, 2009

"I hope you don't do what's easy.
I hope you do what's hard."

JUNE 2, 2006

"What we have already achieved gives us hope for what we can and must achieve tomorrow."

NOVEMBER 4, 2008

"It's up to us — as fathers and parents — to instill this ethic of excellence in our children. It's up to us to say to our daughters, don't ever let images on TV tell you what you are worth, because I expect you to dream without limit and reach for those goals. It's up to us to tell our sons, those songs on the radio may glorify violence, but in my house we give glory to achievement, self respect, and hard work. It's up to us to set these high expectations. And that means meeting those expectations ourselves. That means setting examples of excellence in our own lives."

JUNE 15, 2008

"Now, there are some who question the scale of our ambitions — who suggest that our system cannot tolerate too many big plans. Their memories are short. For they have forgotten what this country has already done; what free men and women can achieve when imagination is joined to common purpose, and necessity to courage."

JANUARY 20, 2009

"In a world that grows smaller by the day, perhaps we can begin to crowd out the destructive forces of zealotry and make room for the healing power of understanding. This is my hope."

FEBRUARY 5, 2009

"We pass on the values of empathy and kindness to our children by living them."

JUNE 15, 2008

"Find somebody to be successful for.
Raise their hopes. Rise to their needs."

MAY 13, 2009

"Instead of driving us apart, our varied beliefs can bring us together to feed the hungry and comfort the afflicted; to make peace where there is strife and rebuild what has broken; to lift up those who have fallen on hard times. This is not only our call as people of faith, but our duty as citizens of America."

FEBRUARY 5, 2009

"I wasn't born with a lot of advantages. But I was given love, and support, and an education that put me on a pathway to success. The same was true for Michelle. She came from a blue-collar family on the South Side of Chicago. Even though her father had multiple sclerosis, he went to work every day at the local water filtration plant to support his family. And Michelle and her brother were able to go to a great college, and reach a little further for their dreams."

SEPTEMBER 9, 2008

REACH

"There is power in words."

"There is power in hope."

FEBRUARY 10, 2007

"We know that the American Dream isn't something that happens to you — it's something you strive for and work for and seize with your own two hands. And we've got a responsibility as a nation to keep that dream alive for all of our people."

AUGUST 2, 2008

"We shouldn't forget that better is not good enough."

MARCH 4, 2007

"This country of ours has more wealth than any nation, but that's not what makes us rich. We have the most powerful military on Earth, but that's not what makes us strong. Our universities and our culture are the envy of the world, but that's not what keeps the world coming to our shores. Instead, it is that American spirit — that American promise — that pushes us forward even when the path is uncertain; that binds us together in spite of our differences; that makes us fix our eye not on what is seen, but what is unseen, that better place around the bend."

AUGUST 28, 2008

"We must find a way to
live together as one
human family."

MAY 17, 2009

"My story is a quintessentially American story. It's the same story that has made this country a beacon for the world — a story of struggle and sacrifice on the part of my forebearers and a story overcoming great odds. I carry that story with me each and every day, it's why I wake up every day and do this, and it's why I continue to hold such hope for the future of a country where the dreams of its people have always been possible."

APRIL 15, 2008

"Don't ever let anyone tell you that change isn't possible. Don't let them tell you that speaking out and standing up against injustice is too risky. What's too risky is keeping quiet. What's too risky is looking the other way."

SEPTEMBER 28, 2007

"We will transform this nation."

OCTOBER 5, 2008

"One voice can change a room. And if a voice can change a room, it can change a city, and if it can change a city, it can change a state, and if it can change a state, it can change a nation, and if it can change a nation, it can change the world."

NOVEMBER 3, 2008

"I know that the only reason Michelle and I are where we are today is because this country we love gave us the chance at an education. And the reason I'm running for President is to give every single American that same chance; to give the young sisters out there born with a gift for invention the chance to become the next Orville and Wilbur Wright; to give the young boy out there who wants to create a life-saving cure the chance to become the next Jonas Salk; and to give the child out there whose imagination has been sparked by the wonders of the internet the chance to become the next Bill Gates."

SEPTEMBER 9, 2008

"We are the hope of those boys who have little; who've been told that they cannot have what they dream; that they cannot be what they imagine.

Yes they can."

DREAM

"Never forget that we have it within our power to shape history in this country."

"My parents shared not only an improbable love; they shared an abiding faith in the possibilities of this nation. They would give me an African name, Barack, or "blessed," believing that in a tolerant America your name is no barrier to success."

JULY 27, 2004

THE GIFT OF HOPE

"The final lesson we must learn as fathers is also the greatest gift we can pass on to our children — and that is the gift of hope."

JUNE 15, 2008

"If there's one thing I've learned in my own life, it's that when you stop listening to the cynics and start trying to make that difference, extraordinary things can happen."

JULY 26, 2007

"Time and again, we've battled back from adversity by recognizing that common stake that we have in each other's success."

SEPTEMBER 29, 2008

"Focusing your life solely on making a buck shows a poverty of ambition. It asks too little of yourself. And it will leave you unfulfilled."

JULY 12, 2006

"**I** can still remember a conversation I had with an older man all those years ago just before I left for Chicago. He said, 'Barack, I'll give you a bit of advice. Forget this community organizing business and do something that's gonna make you some money. You can't change the world, and people won't appreciate you trying. But you've got a nice voice, so you should think about going into television broadcasting. I'm telling you, you've got a future.'

Now, he may have been right about the TV thing, but he was wrong about everything else."

MAY 25, 2008

"No matter what our background or where we come from — each of us has the chance to make it if we try."

SEPTEMBER 20, 2008

"Some like to say this country is divided. But that is not how I choose to see it. . . . I see values that all of us share — values of liberty, equality, and service to a common good and a greater good. I see a flag that we fly with pride."

AUGUST 21, 2007

"If we have the courage to commit to change, the American people can not just seize — but shape — the opportunities of the global economy. Together, we can author our own story."

JUNE 26, 2008

"Hope and change have been the causes of my life."

SEPTEMBER 3, 2007

"If you want to change the world, the change has to happen with you first."

MARCH 4, 2007

"We need to show our kids that you're not strong by putting other people down — you're strong by lifting them up. That's our responsibility as fathers."

JUNE 15, 2008

"While our government can provide every opportunity imaginable for us to serve our communities, it is up to each of us to seize those opportunities. To do our part to lift up our fellow Americans. To realize our own true potential."

MARCH 26, 2009

"As hard as it is for me to be away from my own daughters so much, that's what I think about when I have the chance to tuck them in at night. How I want my daughters — and all our daughters — to have no limits on their dreams, no obstacles to their achievement, no opportunities beyond their reach."

JULY 10, 2008

"Our kids are why you wake up wondering how you'll make a difference."

JULY 5, 2007

"This is our moment. This is our time — to put our people back to work and open doors of opportunity for our kids; to restore prosperity and promote the cause of peace; to reclaim the American Dream and reaffirm that fundamental truth — that out of many, we are one; that while we breathe, we hope, and where we are met with cynicism, and doubt, and those who tell us that we can't, we will respond with that timeless creed that sums up the spirit of a people: Yes We Can."

NOVEMBER 4, 2008

"In this world of competing claims about what is right and what is true, have confidence in the values with which you've been raised and educated. Be unafraid to speak your mind when those values are at stake. Hold firm to your faith and allow it to guide you on your journey. In other words, stand as a lighthouse."

MAY 17, 2009

"I ask you to believe — to believe in yourselves, in each other, and in the future we can build together.

Together, we cannot fail."

OCTOBER 25, 2008

"If we don't try, if we don't reach high, then we won't make any progress."

APRIL 7, 2009

"Even in the hardest times, against the toughest odds, we've never given in to pessimism; we've never surrendered our fates to chance; we have endured; we have worked hard; we sought out new frontiers."

APRIL 27, 2009

PERSEVERE

"That is the true genius of America, a faith in the simple dreams of its people, the insistence on small miracles."

JULY 27, 2004

"We need your service, right now, in this moment — our moment — in history. I'm not going to tell you what your role should be; that's for you to discover."

DECEMBER 5, 2007

"One of my earliest memories is of sitting on my grandfather's shoulders and watching the astronauts come to shore in Hawaii. I remember the cheers and small flags that people waved, and my grandfather explaining how we Americans could do anything we set our minds to do. That's my idea of America."

JUNE 30, 2008

"I think it's time we started putting the health of our families before the profits of our insurance companies."

OCTOBER 5, 2008

"I stand here knowing that my story is part of the larger American story, that I owe a debt to all those who came before me, and that in no other country on Earth is my story even possible."

JULY 27, 2004

"While each of us must do our part, work as hard as we can, and be as responsible as we can — in the end, there are certain things we cannot do on our own. There are certain things we can only do together."

FEBRUARY 12, 2009

"We will make sure that our daughters have the same rights, the same chances, and the same freedoms to pursue their dreams as our sons."

JANUARY 29, 2009

"We'll need to be bold and creative and take risks . . . But that's always been the American story — that belief that all things are possible, that we are limited only by our willingness to take a chance and work hard to achieve our dreams."

MAY 19, 2009

"We exercise our leadership best when we are listening."

APRIL 2, 2009

LEADERSHIP

"If you're walking down the right path and you're willing to keep walking, eventually you'll make progress."

JUNE 13, 2005

"There are few things as fundamental to the American Dream or as essential for America's success as a good education."

APRIL 24, 2009

DREAM

"There's nothing more fundamental than the American Dream."

OCTOBER 23, 2008

"I am not a perfect man and I won't be a perfect president. But my own American story tells me that this country moves forward when we cast off our doubts and seek new beginnings. It's what brought my father across an ocean in search of a dream."

OCTOBER 2, 2007

"Change will not come if we wait for some other person or some other time. We are the ones we've been waiting for. We are the change that we seek."

FEBRUARY 5, 2008

"Find somebody to be successful for. Raise their hopes. Rise to their needs."

MAY, 13, 2009

"I've found that while we may have different stories, we hold common hopes. We may not look the same or come from the same place, but we want to move in the same direction — towards a better future for our children and our grandchildren."

MAY 6, 2008

"**W**hether it's helping to reduce the energy we use, cleaning up a neighborhood park, tutoring in a local school, or volunteering in countless other ways, individual citizens can make a big difference."

MARCH 28, 2009

"There is no destiny that we cannot fulfill."

NOVEMBER 3, 2008

"It's not enough just to look back in wonder of how far we've come — I want us to look ahead with a fierce urgency at how far we have left to go. I believe it's time for this generation to make its own mark — to write our own chapter in the American story."

SEPTEMBER 28, 2007

"The American story has never been about things coming easy — it's been about rising to the moment when the moment was hard. It's about rejecting fear and division for unity of purpose. That's how we've overcome war and depression. That's how we've won great struggles for civil rights and women's rights and workers' rights. And that's how we'll write the next great chapter in the American story."

NOVEMBER 2, 2008

"What makes America's servicemen and women heroes is not just their sense of duty, honor, and country; it's the bigness of their hearts and the breadth of their compassion."

MAY 26, 2008

COURAGE

"This is the moment to begin the work of seeking the peace of a world without nuclear weapons."

JULY 24, 2008

"The future must belong to those who create, not those who destroy."

"I do not accept that the American Dream is a thing of the past."

SEPTEMBER 3, 2007

"I never expected to be here, and I always knew the journey would be improbable. I've never been on one that wasn't."

NOVEMBER 3, 2007

"Hope is not found in any single ideology — an insistence on doing the same thing with the same result year after year. Hope is found in what works."

JULY 18, 2007

"Those of us who have benefited greatly from the blessings of this country have a solemn obligation to open the doors of opportunity, not just for our children, but to all of America's children. That's the kind of vision I have for this country."

FEBRUARY 24, 2008

"When we open up our hearts and our minds to those who may not think precisely like we do or believe precisely what we believe — that's when we discover at least the possibility of common ground."

MAY 17, 2009

"**H**ope is . . . that thing inside that insists, despite all evidence to the contrary, that there are better days ahead. If we're willing to work for it. If we're willing to shed our fears. If we're willing to reach deep inside ourselves when we're tired, and come back fighting harder."

NOVEMBER 3, 2008

"I know the promise of America because I have lived it."

MAY 6, 2008

"Take some risks in your life."

"America is a place where you can make it if you try . . . everyone should have the chance to live their dreams."

SEPTEMBER 29, 2008

"Let us finish the work that needs to be done, and usher in a new birth of freedom on this Earth."

"I ask you to believe —
not just in my ability to
bring about change,
but in yours."

NOVEMBER 3, 2008

"I'm hopeful because I think there's an awakening taking place in America. People are coming together around a simple truth — that we are all connected, that I am my brother's keeper; I am my sister's keeper."

JUNE 23, 2007

"**N**othing worthwhile in this country has ever happened unless somebody, somewhere stood up when it was hard; stood up when they were told — no you can't, and said yes we can."

FEBRUARY 12, 2008

YES WE CAN